Fast Forward to Success

*Break Through Your Limitations
to Change Your
Finances, Family, Fame, Freedom & Future*

Paperback ISBN: 9798408711611
Hardcover ISBN: 9798411894592

FAST FORWARD TO SUCCESS

Break Through
Your Limitations To Change Your
Finances, Family, Fame, Freedom And Future

Pat Mesiti	David Cavanagh	Robin Oliver
Alison Manoukian	Reeta Somerville	Robyn Ius
PJ Ashley	Kerry McKenzie	Erin Beslee
Vicki Stanford	Fololi Lologa	Sylvia Suhr

Chapter 1: Take Big Chances to Chase Your Big Dreams | Fololi Lologa

What are your dreams? I'm not asking about simple wishes or aspirations— I'm asking about your BIG dreams!

I grew up on the tiny Pacific island of Samoa. My mother worked as a school teacher. We didn't have many "outside" financial resources, depending on our crops for income. My parents taught me the foundation of a good education combined with hard work.

I was a big dreamer and set stretch goals for myself, but I had no idea how to reach my destination. I've had to overcome several obstacles and hardships.

I'm an adult educator. I encourage, empower, and help people, just like you, achieve what they set out to achieve. I facilitate learning— if you're not sure where you're going or what you want to achieve, I work with you to draw a map to get you from where you are to where you want to go.

I work with students aged 17 and older, who feel they don't have the skillset, knowledge, or the experience to reach their fullest potential. I help you gain clarity. I sit down and have a conversation about what you want.

My dream was to go to school, get a decent education, earn a degree, and work for the government. I had the opportunity to gain a sponsorship, travel to New Zealand at age 15, and attend college.

Life's Detours

New Zealand was a larger world than I was expecting. I was used to a 120-student school, and was now attending a 1200-student college. I was required to always speak English, but it was my second language. I was also homesick. There was almost no concept of "mental health"— I lacked the assistance I needed.

My first year, I flunked miserably. Since I was abroad, no one understood me the way my teachers did. I wanted to be a schoolteacher and help other "lost" students.

My student visa needed to be renewed every six months, but it was based on my grades. I completed college, but I didn't qualify to continue to university.

I was stuck again. My visa expired. I asked the immigration office, "What do I do? I need my education to achieve this goal." Immigration said, "You're an adult, over 18 years old. You can't get free education anymore. Your sponsorship has completed. You didn't pass your tests. You can return home, and hope for the best."

I was embarrassed. I didn't want to go back as a failure. I asked, "Is there another option?" They said, "If you get a job, you can apply for permanent residence." That was my chance. I obtained the job and paper, but I wasn't satisfied. I wished my career advisor at school had said, "This is what you need to do if you want to go somewhere."

I met my future husband and decided to move to the big city of Auckland. I worked my way from the bottom-up in corporate New Zealand. We grew our charming family of three children. I had no teaching degree, but I homeschooled my children from early childhood to intermediate level.

Ask for Help with Your Big Dreams and Goals

If you don't know where to go and don't know what to do in your life or career, or even business— ask yourself: what are your assets? What can you offer somebody who comes to you for help? Sometimes a student is at a crossroads, completely confused and overwhelmed.

When you don't know what step to take next, ask for help. When I consult with a student, we draw diagrams and lines, from point A to B. We brainstorm, collaborate, and bounce ideas off each other.

For over 20 years, I've taught in a number of faculties at the Institute. Many of my students are preparing for a better job, or are pursuing higher-level education— social work, teaching, or nursing, or business degrees. Over the years, I've met beautiful students, and now I meet most of them in their professional industries.

The COVID-19 Pandemic has disrupted the working environment. Many people have lost jobs. I teach from home.

Make-or-Break Orientation

A middle-aged woman who spent 15+ years in the aviation industry as a cabin crew member with one of the major airlines in Australia and New Zealand lost her job due to COVID. When she approached me for the first time, we sat down for a "make or break" orientation. I asked, "Why do you want to do this? What is your passion?" Having identified her dream job, her passion, we mapped the pathway. I drew a big picture from that first moment to determine how many years it would take to complete her degree.

I said, "This is how long it will take, assuming you pass every level of the program, and graduate on-time with your degree. This is the return on your investment, and this is the cost. It will take this long. Look at where you are and your age. This is the amount of debt you will have at the start of your career. Is this what you want?"

She said, "I'm not sure if I can handle it." This was an entry-level program, level three, or the end of high school. She wasn't completely certain but she asked questions. As the facilitator, educator, lecturer, or teacher, it's my job to listen.

In addition to group support, I provide one-on-one support to my students. They have different ages, experiences, and different educational backgrounds. Some have been at home raising children. While I have a big group, I work on an individual basis to ensure each person handles their individual matters.

I discover your strengths, build confidence, hold your hand, and help you complete your program. I help you overcome your challenge to get you to the next level. I encourage most students to apply for the higher-level program, attend their interview, and complete the assessment.

Learn, Apply, Grow, Inspire

I perform a SWOT analysis to discover the qualities of my students. You can do this too— what are your Strengths, Weaknesses, Opportunities, and Threats?

Take inventory. Own that you're good at "this" skill but not so good at "that." What opportunities can build on those skills? How can you repair your minor weaknesses to improve so your journey can continue?

Add that tool to your toolkit. In the New Zealand Maori language, the word "kete" means a "basket"—

which can mean a "basket of knowledge" or a "basket of tools." Add each tool as you continue.

I love the acronym "LAGI"— Learn, Apply, Grow, Inspire. Will I get this job? Will my career work out? Take the big risk.

Apply for the long-shot job. This can reduce your stress. Suppose you apply for the exact job you want. You're so worried about your future because it hinges on this piece of the plan working out. However, when you apply for the long-shot job and you don't get it, you didn't expect it. If you obtain that long-job shot, there's an unexpected surprise. There's no downside.

Balance Excitement and Emotion with Logic

Dream big. Consider what you would like to be. What's your passion? What's your dream?

Then, apply logic. What work is required to reach the next milestone? What are the steps? How much time is involved based your present age? Calculate the cost and your student loan debt versus your new salary. What's the goal, where are you now, and how do you get from point A to point B?

To recap: put logic aside momentarily, come up with the wild idea, then apply logic. Don't get weighed down by practicality too soon. Allow yourself to consider crazy wild ideas. Use the right tools, at the right time, in the right order, to get where you want to go.

I've navigated many struggles— in my work and personal environment. I've battled perfectionism. My mother, a school teacher, pressured me to score 100% and get A-plus.

I challenge my students: "Go for 100%. If you miss by one point, at least you land on 99%." However, don't go for 50% because if you miss one, you won't pass. Have big dreams, but also create a plan to implement those dreams.

Say Yes to "Why" Now, and Figure Out the "How" Later

I tell my students, "You failed one paper. You didn't fail the entire program. The program is full of different papers. I use the word "failure" sparingly— it has a negative connotation. I say, "I didn't make it. I'll do better next time."

I also don't like the word "difficulty." Don't say, "I have difficulty understanding the paper." Instead, say, "This paper challenges me." If you don't know where to go, you're allowed to take time and walk away temporarily. Get fresh air, come back, sit down, and get to deep thinking.

Understand why you want to do this. Many times, you want to know "how"— but you fail to identify "why." Say "yes" now, and figure out "how" later. Don't say, "I'll think about it." Instead, take the risk.

Fear is not knowing the outcome. However, if you don't take action, you won't know whether the outcome is good or bad, or doesn't turn out the way you want. Figure out the next steps. Know where you are first, and then go from there.

Encouragement & Empowerment

Be prepared for any "surprise" opportunity that was not part of your original plan. For example, I'm building my online education program. I want to encourage and empower someone else to say, "If Fololi can do it, I can do it." You and I may not be on the same exact path, but I have big dreams. I set goals, put an action plan in place, and I work it. I'm not finished. I planned to retire at age 50. I decided to never retire, because I still have a lot to offer.

Who knows what the future holds? I have my "why's." Why am I doing this? For my family— my grandchildren, my current students, and my future students. Who knows what COVID will do to our education system? The only thing that is certain: it's disrupting our work environment, education system, and professional industries. A lot has changed. What was valid 1-2 years ago no longer applies. This coming year, who knows what will happen?

Be prepared for what's ahead of you— mentally, physically, and holistically. Who can you help? Who is there to help you? Focus on what you can do for someone else, and someone else will take care of you and your needs.

Have three goals: personal, professional, and financial. Calculate the steps. Before drilling down into logic, expand your horizon. Dream big and don't be shy to share your dream.

Choose who to include in your dream. Include good support people with you. If you are struggling with your future education, career, and business path— you lack clarity— happy to sit down with you to work on your goals and dreams.

Believe in yourself. Don't stop dreaming. Dream big. Know your "Why." Locate the person that will help you get there.

About Fololi Lologa

Fololi Lologa is an inspirational, motivational, and devoted lecturer, coach and mentor in the tertiary education sector in Aotearoa, New Zealand.

She worked her way up in the NZ corporate ladder for 20 years before landing a lecturing role at the Manukau Institute of Technology where she works with adult students to find clarity, strategies and foundational steps to pursue higher level education or land their dream career and professional roles. If you are starting out or at a crossroad of a career change, Fololi will help you get clarity on your life's calling, purpose, dreams, goals and aspirations. Discover more at FololiLologa.com/offer.

Chapter 2: Evolve Into the Person You Were Meant to Become Through Hard Work, Skill-Building, and Problem-Solving | Robyn Ius

You can learn to manage the technical aspects of your website at any age or stage of life.

Let me explain. I am a creative person, and my first career choice was an artist. I followed that theme through university from the age of 16. I studied drawing, painting, printmaking, and fine-art photography. The problem: I couldn't see a career path with my artwork since I didn't want to teach at that time. I believed my best option was photography. I landed a commercial photographic job, and after a few years, I decided to pursue a role in portrait photography.

This suited me. I trained every weekend and assisted in photographing weddings for free for twelve months before landing my first wedding to shoot.

A Dream Come True, Or Was It?

That first wedding did not quite go as planned. As the bride walked down the aisle, I discovered that the bracket that held my flash was broken. A tiny pin had fallen out in my camera case. When I picked up the flash bracket to attach it to the camera, it would not stay connected.

There's not a lot of room for mistakes in weddings. If you have a mishap, you can quickly lose a critical shot. There are no rewinds at a live event. Quick thinking was required! I thanked the heavens that first day because I had a young assistant who could hold my flash as we walked down the aisle. We were virtually joined at the hip as the cord from the camera to flash was relatively short. We probably looked odd, but maybe no one noticed. In any case, it was such a relief I didn't miss a shot!

To make this an enjoyable career, I learned to have options for the unexpected. This was a great learning experience that would help me in the future. I thrived in the creative space of wedding photography — directing bridal parties and family members into poses to enhance the imagery for their special day. I started my own business and continued successfully for eighteen years.

The digital era came in, and cameras changed every year. I avoided the change because, at the time, I didn't think I could evolve into this new technology. So, I continued shooting with film, as did 50% of the photographers in Melbourne.

I ended my photographic career because of the physicality of the job. I didn't want to lug heavy equipment around a church and park, not seeing my family on weekends and evenings. One evening, I was walking back to my car after finishing a wedding in the Botanical Gardens in Melbourne. I didn't have an assistant that day, so I had to carry all my gear. I had a small ladder, a heavy metal case, a reflector and a tripod.

I felt so exhausted and found each step carrying all the gear so painful. After taking a few steps, I put the camera case down to rest. I found myself crying as I walked across the park to get to my car. That was the moment I decided to find another career. It's a challenging place to drop everything you know after a long season and take up a different job, but that's precisely what I did.

Can An Artistically Minded Person Learn to Be a Technical Guru?

I enjoyed editing photographs and creating beautiful portraits to impress my clients. It was satisfying to hear my customers express sheer delight as they viewed their images. Still, I had to wean myself off this space and look for another career path.

Websites weren't prevalent in 1996. There were only 100,000 sites at the time. Most people had dial-up connections, which took forever to connect to the internet. However, by 2008, there were 160 million sites. That's how quickly it grew.

To the uninitiated like me, a website looked like a pretty picture on a computer. I was inquisitive and wanted to create them myself. I signed up for a web design course at the local university. I remember the row of beautiful looking Mac computers in that classroom.

I was terrified. I didn't even know how to turn one on. One person in the class seemed to have a grip on HTML. Many students asked him for help. With all his expertise and guru status, he didn't present a website at the end of term because his files were too large— the computer couldn't cope, and he gave up.

Good Old-Fashioned Tenacity

As a mature age student, I had one thing going for me: good old-fashioned tenacity to get the job done. The first time I needed to present something to the class, I was in a tither. The presentation computer was situated in the middle of the classroom. The room was full of young people waiting to see my presentation. It was so intimidating I wondered whether I could even locate the slot to insert my portable drive.

I panicked. Could I find my project with all eyes on me? Would my verbal presentation be coherent? I knew the lecturer would be giving me an immediate grade in front of the class. It was a terrifying ordeal.

My thoughts paralyzed me on the inside. You can imagine how relieved I was to complete my presentation. Based on the marks and comments, I did very well.

At the end of the year, I was asked to join a full-time course. I thought, "I could go back to school full-time." The advanced diploma in web design was full, so I needed other options. I joined the engineering department and embarked on a full-time study in computer science— web development. Me, the creative artist in the engineering department!

That first day, I realized I had missed an introductory course: how to pull a computer apart. Being a mature age student, I was not given a tour of the university and the full prospectus of the course. I felt behind the eight ball.

When I arrived in my class to study C# programming, I thought, "Is this for me? I can't understand anything they're talking about." It sounded like math and formulas. I removed the programming subjects and focused only on web development: HTML, CSS, PHP, MySQL, and JavaScript.

There were a couple of mature-aged students in the class, but most were young people. At least one principal lecturer was biased toward looking after the young students. When it was my time to get assistance, it didn't matter if I waved my hand all day, no one was coming. I had to work incredibly hard to understand the concepts. I learned how my brain functions. I prefer to have the big picture of what I'm doing before diving into the details. You need to understand how you learn best.

Hard Work Pays Off

In the final year of the course, we created a real-life project. Many projects were for external companies. One involved software that saved the lives of helicopter pilots.

I didn't get on that team but found myself project manager for a student portal that the university would use. It was exciting to work on something that would be used in real life. Part of the project required a bug (error) checker. We were told to use the best student bug checker software we created the previous year.

As the project manager, I approached the lecturer to determine who made the best bug-checker software. There were brilliant young software developers in the class, and I guessed it would belong to one of them. However, the lecturer said it was mine! I thought he was lying to me. He explained that mine was the only one completed that worked.

What a surprise! I learned to not doubt myself. I had more to offer as a mature student than I realized. I could achieve my goals. That year, I completed the student portal, gained successful marks, a diploma in web development, and the prospect of a new career.

Within a year, I became employed full-time as a web developer and content creator. Starting a new role as a web developer and content creator was a learning experience. I had significant responsibilities.

My primary responsibility was to manage 150 websites. My boss tested me to see if I could fix the JavaScript problems and passed that successfully. The other part of the role included teaching admin staff how to look after their website, over the phone. Some people couldn't find their website address or password, let alone the images they needed to add to their site.

20

I could walk people through the steps, and enjoyed listening to their small successes. I had the patience to discover their biggest fears and difficulties. The years of battling my own digital fears helped me put myself in their shoes and understand their thought patterns. I transformed my fears into an advantage.

I was given the opportunity to continue my studies: a diploma in digital marketing. I was already doing marketing in the role but making it formal was a significant step. Out of the many aspects of marketing, search engine optimization fascinated me the most.

The Art & Science of SEO

SEO (search engine optimization) means improving aspects of your website to bring it to the front of the search engine results page so it can be seen by the most people possible. It's an imperfect art because of the algorithms or 200 ranking factors, which change daily. The key is to stay abreast of changes and cover the basics.

The most important ranking factor is to look after your website users by giving them a great website experience. All pictures, buttons and forms must load within three seconds. Ensure your visitors can find the information or content they require. Provide the keywords a Google Search Bot needs to match the user's search intent.

When you write content for your page, consider if it is helpful to your user. It must have the keywords this user would type in the search browser. They need to appear in functional areas such as the URL, title, headings and paragraphs. Having a YouTube video on your page can improve your ranking. There are over 200 ranking factors. Check off the ones you can. That will give you a head start over other competitors.

Some factors require a continual concerted effort. The age of your site is a factor. The popularity of your site is a significant ranking factor. Give more than the user expects, so other websites will link to yours since they find the content beneficial and trustworthy.

As backlinks build up, they are given a score out of 100 called the Domain Authority. The domains linking to your domain must also be reputable and popular. Create popular, valuable pages that work efficiently and in a way that makes robots and your users find them.

I fully understand how people might feel in grappling with this ever-evolving digital world. My experiences and journey to get where I am will aid in helping you grasp the concept of SEO and how to maximize your business online. If I can do it, you can too.

About Robyn Ius

Robyn is a trained artist, photographer, web developer/designer, content creator and SEO marketer with 33 years of business experience. She ran her own photography business for 18 years and now runs a successful web design business in Melbourne, Victoria.

Robyn empowers you to Audit your Online Business and Create a website that Floods with Free traffic Without paying Thousands a Month on SEO. Claim her free offer: Three must-have items for great website SEO, including essential Website Speed, Keywords and Indexing. Get your Free Mini SEO course: SeeTheVision.com.au/seo/mini-seo.

Chapter 3: Help Your Child Cross the Bridge to Literacy | Erin Beslee

As a parent, you want your child to be successful in life and reach their full potential. As they get closer in age to starting school, you wonder what you can do to help your child's learning, to give them a head start.

You and I know how to read and write and take these skills for granted. They're essential skills for living in today's modern world. As the parent of a young child, you recognize the importance of learning to read and write. Literacy equals the freedom to make choices in life.

As an Early Childhood Teacher working in community-based preschools in Sydney for over twenty years, I'm often asked by parents, "How can I teach my child to read? I want them to be top of the class when they start school." "Some of the mothers at playgroup have signed up for a particular reading program. Which one do you recommend?" "Should I enroll my child in a reading class? I've heard they're very good!"

Expensive reading programs aren't necessary. Early language and literacy experiences with meaningless drills and repetitious routines are boring for young children, especially when they have no contextual relevance. Phonics programs, flashcards, workbooks and watered-down school curriculums are not appropriate. What is important is that your child has the ability to concentrate long enough to listen to a story, and is *read to* on a regular basis.

Your Child Can't Learn to Read If They Aren't Read To

I often ask parents, "Do you read to your child at home?" I'm amazed how many parents answer:

- "No, we don't have time."
- "I finish work too late."
- "My child already gets to bed too late most nights as it is."
- "We tried that and it doesn't work for our family."

Your child can't learn to read if they aren't read to. The fewer words your child experiences, learns, and uses before school, the more difficulties they will encounter.

Professor Pamela Snow at La Trobe University, Melbourne states, "A five-year-old needs a lot of linguistic capital in place in terms of their vocabulary, knowledge of the world, exposure to stories and complex sentences before they are ready to cross the bridge into literacy."

Mem Fox, internationally respected literacy expert and author of numerous well-known and much-loved children's books tells us that, "Words are essential in building the thought connections in the brain. The more language a child experiences, the more advanced socially and educationally that child will be for the rest of their life."

I've observed the approaches parents take to help their children learn to read, some successful, others ending in tears. There are pitfalls and mistakes to avoid.

Sam's Struggle

One little boy's parents were eager to accelerate his learning prior to attending school. They decided "reading" was the obvious skill to focus on.

Sam (not his real name) was a quiet-natured four-year-old with a happy disposition. Sam came from a household where everything evolved around sports. His parents were involved in numerous community sporting activities, and Sam wanted to be just like them.

Sam enjoyed preschool, playing outdoors, expending his energy on the climbing equipment and chasing his friends in the playground, but when it came to sitting with his classmates on the mat to listen to his teacher read a book, he preferred to play with trains or build with Legos. He didn't want to sit on the mat. He had no intention of listening to the story.

Sam found it difficult during routine times. Reading was an enjoyable experience for many of his friends, but Sam needed encouragement to sit with a book. Books held no interest. Sometimes he would sit with his teacher and a small group of children, listening to a story just long enough to see what the other children were doing, and would run off.

Sam became eager to sit with his peers at preschool and listen to a story being read. He showed a growing interest in books, especially ones about dinosaurs. He'd choose a book to "read" with friends during free play, and on occasion he'd sit quietly by himself with a book, while his peers engaged in other activities.

Six months prior to starting school Sam's parents enrolled him in a weekly reading class and purchased flashcards (a card with, for example, a picture of a ball with the word "ball" written next to it). Sam was shown the cards and asked to name each picture.

One day, at preschool, Sam's mother excitedly told me she'd caught Sam looking at a book at home in his bedroom. She proudly exclaimed, "I was so excited I rang Sam's dad at work to tell him." Sam didn't understand. He was doing what had become an everyday experience at preschool. Sam's body language told me he was embarrassed. He didn't understand the significance of what looking at a book at home meant to his mother and father.

Sam's enthusiasm to participate in literacy experiences at preschool waned. Sam was far from enjoying the occasions when flashcards were pulled out. He didn't enjoy his reading class.

He's Not the Happy Little Boy He Used to Be

Sam's mother told me she'd bought some phonics and reading activity books for Sam. Each day after breakfast he was encouraged to engage in these activities before being allowed outside to play.

Sam had been attending school for several months when his mother told me Sam was struggling. She couldn't understand why he didn't want to go to school. "He loved preschool, but now he is disruptive, distracted, won't do homework, and isn't advancing. He's not the happy little boy he used to be!"

Sam had decided he didn't like books or reading. You can't blame him. In his short life, learning to read was far from enjoyable. Consider the emotions you feel when you attempt to understand the tax code or your ideal health plan. Sam's disruptive behavior at school resulted from him avoiding reading-related activities.

If a child doesn't see reading as fun, something that has meaning and something they can achieve, why would they want to engage in it? If joy has been replaced with feelings of dread, what goes through their minds when they get to school? Do you think they'll be excited and willing to learn, or will they turn off, tune out and be disruptive in class?

The Domino Effect

Many children have traveled similar paths to Sam's: they're expected to participate in some formal training but have not learned the early foundations. Their parents want them to walk before they can crawl. Infants need to crawl before they can walk, before they can run. Learning to read is no different.

Unfortunately, Sam's parents, as well meaning as they were in teaching Sam to read, unwittingly short-changed their little boy. Sam will continue to struggle, and his entire future may be impacted.

Research by Professor Snow has found that poor reading and writing feeds the school-to-prison pipeline, a pathway that starts when students struggle in the early years of school. "They struggle and start to fall behind, and often their behavior becomes problematic. Before long, they are missing school and hanging out with other disengaged peers. Underachieving becomes the norm. Then they are knocking off cars, and you can see where the school-to-prison pipeline comes from." Professor Snow also points out that social marginalization, while not literally a prison, is a chronic and painful form of social exclusion. In a recent study she found that 87% of a sample of youth offenders in New South Wales had experienced school suspensions and expulsions.

Failure is Painful & Self Esteem Starts to Erode

In an article titled 'Can't Read? Go Directly to Jail. Do Not Pass Go', US Reading Specialist, Judy Santilli Packhem writes, "If a child doesn't achieve success at reading in the early grades, he will not even want to attempt it, because failure is painful. Self esteem starts to erode. The non-reader feels shame. He doesn't want anyone to know he can't read. He refocuses the attention. He begins to misbehave. It is better to get in trouble for misbehaving than to risk other kids knowing you can't read. The misbehavior becomes a pattern and escalates into crime. I realize this is an extreme oversimplification. But the truth of it is there. 85% of all juveniles in the US juvenile court system are functionally illiterate."

The early years of a child's life are important in shaping their entire lives. Early childhood is such an important time for laying the foundations on which ALL future learning is based. This statement is substantiated by neuroscientists worldwide. Brain research tells us that the crucial connections in the young child's brain get excited and go off like fireworks when stimulated through playful learning experiences. We all recognize that infants and young children are like little sponges, constantly absorbing information about the world around them. They're learning all the time and with every new piece of information and stimulation critical connections in the brain are enhancing and determining their future learning outcomes.

You can begin to instill a love of reading in your child from birth, or even while they're in the womb. It's never too early, and it's never too late, to support your child's reading ability. You don't need formal qualifications. You only need to have fun together reading aloud regularly. Not a rushed, clock-watching or answering the phone between pages experience, but one where you are both relaxed and enjoying the time spent together. Your child will learn from every occasion when you read aloud to them. Make the time you spend together fun. Begin reading a well-loved book upside down, or from the back page. You'll be engulfed in a sea of squeals of laughter and delight when your child corrects you. Their response to your "mistake" will signal that they're learning to read by simply being read to. They're learning by osmosis!

Gift the Love of Reading

The child who arrives at school with strong pre-literacy foundations will have enjoyed a plethora of playful learning experiences with stories, illustrations, words and print and they'll be enthusiastic to participate in class. They'll enjoy listening to stories being read by the teacher and they'll have fun exploring rhyming words and the repetition of words, silly, nonsensical words, all of which are building their vocabulary and understanding of and familiarity with print. They'll understand the role that illustrations play. They'll learn that words on the pages relate to the pictures. They'll be full of confidence to build on their existing early literacy skills. They'll be ready to take on board the teacher's instruction and experience the pleasure and excitement of reading books.

A love of reading will open up limitless opportunities for your child to expand their knowledge, their understanding of the world and, more importantly as Einstein would say, their imagination. If your child has a lively imagination they'll become a creative thinker, a problem solver, and the world will be their oyster as creative thinking skills will no doubt be essential going into the future.

Many parents set up a trust fund for their child's future education. Why not invest a small amount of time, as little as fifteen minutes a day, to read aloud to your child? Gift them a love of reading that will last their lifetime. Whether you're a single parent, time poor family, grandparent, aunty or uncle, the child in your life will have fond memories of the fun you had reading together, and the bond that you'll establish will astound you. Your life, and theirs, will be enriched beyond words.

About Erin Beslee

Erin is a university qualified Early Childhood Teacher who graduated from Charles Sturt University, Bathurst. She has worked with children aged 3-5 years in community-based preschools in Sydney for the past 20+ years. She is passionate about seeing every child reach their full potential. Erin's teaching experience has given her insight into how young children can read without a single lesson being taught. Play is the answer.

Go to ErinBeslee.com to download the FREE 3-part video series, "The 3 Little-Known Secrets To Ensure Your Young Child's Reading Success."

Chapter 4: Be a World Changer | Sylvia Suhr

Have you ever stopped to think about the God who placed you here, at this moment in time, with the people He's put in your life?

You and I fit into His plan, even if we don't see the how or why.

What does it take for you to become a world-changer?

Being single, a woman, over seventy, might sound like good reasons not to follow God in amazing adventures. I can assure you that there are no excuses. **A life surrendered to God is the greatest adventure you could ever imagine.**

Who would believe that someone like me would be able to touch and change the lives of so many people? An ordinary girl, coming from humble beginnings but growing up to live a life of unexpected and remarkable experiences.

I was born at the end of the Second World War in Stoke-on-Trent, an industrial town in the middle of England. Tall chimneys and terraced-type houses in long rows graced clean-curtained windows as if competing for "best dressed."

My life was a journey through hardships and joys which helped me to discover myself through amazing experiences. I have healed and found the freedom to become the person I always knew lived inside of me.

As I grew in confidence and inner strength, I was able to bring encouragement and hope to many people I met, in many places around the world.

For the past 21 years, I have traveled to many parts of Africa and Asia, often visiting remote villages, living amongst the people, sometimes for several years at a time.

Hardships, Joys & Miracles

I have rescued orphans from devastating situations in remote villages in Kenya and Malawi and helped them to discover their potential through a loving environment and good schooling. Many of these children are now in high school and university. They

40

have dreams to become doctors, nurses, engineers, and entrepreneurs.

I rode on the back of bicycles and motorcycles to provide medical supplies in remote villages, providing money and food for people in extremely demanding situations. I sometimes met locals who said I was the first white missionary to live in the area.

I loved spending time with Cosmos, who was 107 years old. He had served in two world wars, and had walked where Jesus walked in Israel. He didn't speak a word of English, but we were able to communicate through an interpreter.

We witnessed many amazing miracles. Malaria healed instantly, a man on death's doorstep recovered from AIDS, even the dead raised to life.

One day, I was walking with one of the pastors. We saw a man standing over a lady by the side of the road. The man seemed distressed, was holding his head, and screaming. There was a bicycle by his side he had been using to transport the lady to the clinic.

As we came closer, we saw that the woman seemed unconscious. Her eyes were up in her head and fixed.

We prayed for the woman. The pastor commanded the spirit of death to leave her. I was rubbing her face. Her eyes flickered and she regained consciousness. They continued to the clinic. We never saw them again, but we believe that a miracle had taken place, and she was alive. As we walked away, I asked, "Did that really happen?" It was like we had been in a dream.

Salvation

In Manila (Philippines), I spent 10 weeks at Smoky Mountain. This was a large landfill, a 50-meter-high mountain of garbage, and more than 2 million tons of waste. Plastic bags, bottles, tires, cardboard compressed together. It was hard to keep my eyes open because of the smoke and stench.

I've lived in Tondo, one of the most impoverished areas in the world. Thousands of people built homes out of cardboard and scrap materials. Cockroaches were the size of a large cucumber slice. Rats as big as cats. Mothers sitting on their doorsteps combing their children's hair to remove head lice. Groups of children run around and happily played.

We visited people living in shacks at the rubbish dump and prayed for their needs. Many accepted the salvation message, and we saw people's lives transformed by the power of God as we shared the love of God with each one. We set up a program for nutritional feeding for children. Many had worms, which they expelled within a few days on the nutritional program. Their bodies took in nourishment from the daily cup of nutritional milk.

God Provides

The pastor was helping people set up small businesses with micro finances from a donor in England. Many built businesses, bringing them out of poverty. The pastor obtained a loan and began a small business from his home at Smokey Mountain.

After the first month, the ministry slowed down because of the hot weather, which was unbearable during the day. We spent many hours in prayer and fasting. By the end of two months, I decided my work was finished. It would be good to return to Australia. We said our goodbyes, and I was on my way home.

God revealed Himself to me. My life was transformed as I surrendered to Jesus to do his will. **God has provided for me in so many miraculous ways that I could never have imagined.**

There was a time when I was planning to go to Malawi to work with a pastor. I set a date, October 30th, and started making plans to leave. I very rarely have the money for my missions to overseas countries, but God shows me to walk by faith. He always provides. Close to the time I was to leave, a friend called to ask when I would return to Africa. October 30th. He said he had money and would like to send me a gift. I was amazed! Within a week, I received a check for over $2,000, which helped with the cost of my plane ticket.

You and I serve a God who never fails us when we trust Him and walk by faith, knowing that He is good and faithful.

Get Out There, Take Action, Do Your Part & Change Lives

I arrived back in Kenya, and my new friend Joshua was at the airport in Nairobi to meet me. We chatted about our families and our expectations and visions most of the way to Homa Bay.

We arrived in Shauri Yako, where I was to stay. This was a slum area with great opportunities for evangelism. We hired a videographer and organized a team to preach the gospel door-to-door in the community. People in the area were incredibly open to the simple gospel message we preached. 150 people prayed for salvation that day.

We prayed for many sick people and saw the power of God in action. Many testified that pain had left their bodies.

One lady was lying on a dirt floor in a tin shed. After we prayed for her, we returned after a few days to take food. We cleaned the house, bought her a new bed, and organized people to ensure she was properly cared for. We heard she died recently, but at least we know she received salvation, received personal care, and realized that she was loved.

Joshua told me about his home, Buche Village. I was eager to visit his family. When we arrived, it had not rained for some time— it looked very dry and barren. Rain clouds were building as we arrived, so we visited the village locals, who lived in mud huts with no electricity or toilet facilities. Paraffin lamps were used for lighting, wood and charcoal for cooking. Women carried water in large containers on their heads, obtained from a hand-operated pump.

The first people we met were Joshua's mother and aunt. They were dressed in clothes that showed they belonged to a local cult. They were not yet saved. They received the gospel message, and his mother removed her headdress after praying for salvation.

Spread Your Message & Unlock the Door to Your Potential

We visited many houses. Most of the people had never heard the gospel message. They were eager to receive salvation and hear more about our teachings. The next day, rain poured down, so we were unable to visit them. To our surprise, many people instead visited our house, where we were staying. They asked about our message, then prayed for salvation.

We were in the village for six days. Ten people visited the house each day to receive the gospel. One day, a ladies' group of 25 women visited us. Only four ladies said they were saved. We had a glorious time preaching the gospel and leading others in prayer for salvation, with rejoicing and singing.

It was time to leave Buche Village, and we realized over 100 people had prayed for salvation during the week we were there. It was difficult for us to leave the village, as it had rained.

They managed to find gumboots for me. We returned to Homa Bay tired but happy that God had demonstrated His amazing grace and favor.

My time in Malawi was so exciting. We visited remote villages and saw many people receive salvation and healing. We went as far as the border of Mozambique where they grow much of the rice in Malawi. This is the primitive Africa I love so much, with mud huts and pit latrines, where children and many adults have never seen white people before. Many children run away screaming. Others have big grins with rows of white teeth and want to touch our skin and feel the difference.

Discover and Live the Life God Has Ordained For You

You have enormous potential stored inside you, waiting to be discovered and developed. You could have the key to someone's development, recognize and unlock doors that have been locked in people's lives through disappointment, rejection, or embarrassment.

You could awaken God-given gifts in the lives of people with words of encouragement that could have a lasting influence on their lives.

Surrender your life to God by believing in His way of salvation. Romans 3:23 explains that everyone has sinned and fallen short of the glory of God. But God, in His great love, sent His own Son from heaven to die on the cross in our place. God loves you and He gave Himself for you. There was no other way to resolve this serious sin issue that everyone faces.

In John 14:6 Jesus said, "I am the way, the truth, and the life. No one can come to the Father except through Me."

Romans 10:9,10... "If you confess with your mouth the Lord Jesus and believe in your heart that God has raised Him from the dead, you will be saved. For with the heart, one believes unto righteousness and with the mouth, confession is made unto salvation."

Salvation comes not merely by believing that Jesus is the Son of God, but by receiving Him into your life.

You can say a prayer like this: "God, I know that I am a sinner. I repent of going my own way. Right now, I turn from my sin and ask you to come into my life. I surrender my life to you and put my faith in Jesus Christ. Thank you for loving me and dying for me. In Jesus name, I pray."

Do What Your Inner Voice Tells You to Do

Ask God to lead you to people who will help you to get to know God better and hear His voice. When you receive salvation, Jesus takes residence in your heart and you become like Him.

Be obedient to His still, small voice. Jesus said, "My sheep will know my voice and they follow me." Don't worry about the consequences. You will be amazed at the possibilities as you step out in faith. **Sometimes you need to do it scared.** Each time you face your fears, you become more confident. New experiences will make your life rich and exciting.

Read the Bible, especially the New Testament. The book of John helps you see Jesus through the eyes of love. Being a Christian is not just knowing about God. It's about knowing God Himself and surrendering your will moment by moment. Day by day.

Many people who achieve their dreams are not extraordinary. God doesn't call the qualified, but He qualifies those He has called.

Those that God has called never stop believing in their dreams, in themselves, and in the amazing God who created them.

About Sylvia Suhr

Sylvia Suhr is a published author and a missionary/evangelist who has a passion to see people come to know the saving love of Christ. She travels the world, carrying the message of salvation, giving hope to thousands of people.

Sylvia's book and its personal narrative take you on an adventure into England, Africa, and Australia— into the lives of ordinary people, transforming them to know that God has a special plan for them.

Come on this magic carpet ride as you read of how to steal treasures out of the darkness. Treasures in earthen vessels. Visit SylviasDream.com.

Chapter 5:
Supernatural Success
| Reeta Somerville

Where is your ship traveling? Your ship is your body, your mind, your spirit and your destiny.

Your life is like a ship sailing on the high seas of mysteries until you reach your destiny. These mysteries include how God chose where you would be born, your parents, childhood surroundings, relationships, circumstances and the people we meet until you reach your desired haven.

I have been a registered nurse for 20 years, working with hundreds of neonatal patients and their families. It has been rewarding helping tiny babies to grow and have emergency skills in those terrible emergency situations when I have prayed and hoped for miracles. I have enjoyed holding little hands and stroking little feet. I've encouraged mothers and fathers during difficult hospital stays.

I enjoy working together towards the goal of maintaining a precious life with a great team. My work has made a difference in many lives.

Challenges vs. Stress

Hospital work can be challenging. Countless night duties, staying up all night feeding little tummies, ensuring breathing function and ensuring hearts were pumping efficiently. Exhausting work where double shifts were standard. My brain felt overstimulated, my body exhausted, my mood altered. I fasted overnight, only tea and coffee throughout night duty, just to keep going.

I was often moody and depressed. Research shows that employees working overnight cut their life span as much as 10 years. I began exercising to keep myself fit and mentally motivated for my work requirements.

To continue being promoted in a hospital environment, one needs further qualifications or to establish great relationships with upper management. I faced many obstacles climbing the ladder.

I was a foreigner in Australia who spoke in a funny accent. I had studied overseas, and lacked leadership experience.

Stuck in the Same Old Pattern

I was stuck doing what I had always been doing, the same-old-same-old pattern. I applied for many positions, only to be given another refusal based on various reasons. "Never-quite-good-enough" was my old mindset. Something called me to arise, shine, and take charge of my destiny. I was still young and healthy. I had another 25 years of work ahead of me.

Working for an organization means to abide by their rules within your scope of practice. In nursing, the Australian Health Practitioner Regulation Agency and Employer creates rules and policies regarding the scope of practice. By following their rules, you get to keep your registration and your job. It is beneficial for safety purposes and organizational management, but when it becomes controlling measurement, you are suffocated— losing your personal freedom and independence. Most medical professionals want to help patients and stay out of politics.

I faced the choice of injecting an unknown substance into my body, against my belief and medical knowledge, or letting go of my cherished profession. I had trained for years to be professional and was passionate about miracle patients. I felt like I was losing my experience and my good income. I felt depressed, sad and indecisive. I was angry that I had to make this decision.

For months, I was "hiding" at work— trying to be invisible and not to engage in conversations about this hideous mandate. I worked more night duties to be invisible and avoid ridicule for my opinions. I avoided my friends, who seemed to be against me. A friend asked, "Why don't you want to protect your patients and be a responsible nurse? Why can't you be a good citizen and comply with citizenship duties?" I would not attend functions because of the fear of being ridiculed for my decision.

One day, there was a deadline. I had to tell my manager I would not participate in an unknown vaccination trial. I had endured enough of being upset and emotional. It was my time to stand up and pick up the courage deep within me.

This is Your Time to Succeed

What in *your* life needs changing? Now is your time to make a change. Your time is precious. You will never get it back. Lost time is never found again.

This is YOUR time to shine and make a difference!

I had to let go of my job so that I could get something new. When one door closes, another one opens.

Let go of the past! Don't cry about what was lost. Look to the amazing future ahead of you. Open your eyes to new opportunities.

What has wounded you? A relationship, financial loss, undesired job, illness, loss of health? You may be feeling depressed, anxious, pain or fear deep inside.

Symbolically, it is like an arrow tipped inside you, pulling you down with extra weight. Carrying extra weight makes you a lousy marathon runner in life. When your legs get tired, run with your heart.

I have experienced opposition from my colleagues, friends and family members. I have not received the support I longed for. They did not understand why I "wasted" my medical professional career for my own personal beliefs. It is painful, hurtful and causes depression, low mood and sleeplessness.

Pull out the arrow that is still sore inside of you. Forgiveness means acknowledging someone's bad behavior, validating the pain and moving forward. Hand it over to God and expect to heal the wound.

Don't believe those who talk bad about you. They say "you're a loser", "you're too young", "you're too old", or other excuses and reasons for not being good enough.

But you *are* good enough! No matter who is against you, God is on your side. He will never forsake you.

You are better, smarter, more beautiful, more loved, more capable, and stronger than you think!

I could have stayed at my job and acted against my core beliefs. It was time to live by faith, follow my heart, and trust my financial, emotional, physical and relational needs would be met. I prayed and meditated more. I looked after myself by exercising and eating healthily. I looked for other work options, related to my "health" passion. It is amazing what happens when you open your eyes to new possibilities, pull your head out of the sand, and look around.

Life is Worth Living

I felt lonely after I finished working— my job environment at the hospital was very social and interactive. I created new and wonderful relationships by encouraging friends with the same vision and mindset. I felt freedom flooding into my life.

What does freedom look like for you? Freedom is how you choose your time and whom you spend your time with. Cherish positive people and abandon negative people. Negative people know what they don't want, but positive people know what they want. Choose to think positively about what you want.

I felt alive. Every bone and muscle in my body celebrates life. My mind is clear. I have so much energy. I believe the future will be good. I have always prayed to my heavenly Father and believed that God will help, no matter what comes against me in the natural world.

I could have said to myself " I am nothing", "I can't do this", "I have never done it before", "I'm too old", or "I'm too sick." Instead, I said and thought, "Gee, I can do this. I will be okay. I can make a difference in the world to other people. I matter."

Choose positive words over your feelings, as you wage war against your old mindset.

The Car Accident

We were recently in a car accident. Our family was returning home from a relaxing beach holiday. On a roundabout, a vehicle stopped in front of us. My husband was looking to the right and decided to move, but the car in front did not move. We hit the other car. The other driver did not bother stopping and drove off.

In a situation like this, there are two choices to make.

You can react with words like shouting, using not-so-nice words. Or, you can respond with your words and positive thinking. This requires self-control, patience and perhaps biting your tongue, but it is doable.

I was annoyed, but we decided to think positively. We decided to be grateful that our family was not injured. We were grateful we could still drive home instead of being towed away. We were grateful we had an insurance policy that would cover the cost of repairs.

In the end, the insurance company decided to pay out the whole value of the car.

Imagination Creates What You Desire

By visualizing and speaking out words— the building blocks of your imagination— and believing, you can manifest "things" on earth. God created the world, by His spoken word. The supernatural magic still works. According to the bible, God works in mysterious ways. What the devil meant for evil, God will turn it out for our good.

After the car accident, we needed a new car. This meant letting go of memories of the old car and imagining the new car.

When you let go of something in your mind, you create more space to imagine, to have a vision and to dream.

My husband wanted a white, four-wheel-drive pick-up truck with a turbocharged direct injection diesel engine with leather seats. He wanted it for his business and to take our son for motor-cross-training with bikes in the back. We received our brand new, white Volkswagen Amarok within 6 weeks of the accident, a miracle, because the normal waiting period was three months. We were blessed beyond our imagination!

Hope Beyond the Horizon

I started to fulfill my dream of seeing people healed without medication. My passion for health could be utilized in a different way than what I had imagined.

I began learning new skills in areas: computer work, writing a book, designing my website and creating my own business. The puzzle pieces started to come together piece by piece.

My life is content and abundantly full with gratitude, love, hope and peace. I want to share good news to everyone I meet. God has changed my life.

I want to help you to do the same. There is hope beyond the horizon. I want to pray for you and be your personal health coach. Together, we can make you successful in what you desire to do.

New Adventures Are Waiting

You can make a difference and live the life you want. No one else can do it for you. You have the keys to open up the doors to your destiny. Open the sealed box to your freedom.

Failing in something new isn't an option for me anymore. I have failed before, but this time it will not be a failure. Those who don't get up again are failures. Do not take failure personally. It does not define you.

Make a quality decision not to be fearful about anything. Your unconscious mind kicks in when you sleep and it can be hard to rest when afraid. Remember that fear is not a good advisor. Do not listen to your inner fear but instead your inner faith.

God has not blessed you with fear but with faith, inner power, extraordinary love and clear mind.

New adventures in your life are waiting to be fulfilled. Be brave. Choose life, not death. Take courage, not discourage. Have faith— not fear— in yourself and God. Never lose your hope in getting what you want. Take charge of your natural God-given immunity, health and destiny.

Where do you want to travel? **Let's do it together!**

About Reeta Somerville

Reeta is a Neonatal Nurse Specialist with over 20 years of experience in a major Hospital setting as a Neonatal Nurse Specialist, gifted in the area of healing and natural medicine, an  author, a business owner, a parent with two teens, married to her high school sweetheart.

She is committed to helping you implement a program with proven principles and strategies to achieve better health and natural immunity through her 5-step program in holistic wellness, at ReetaSomerville.com/offer.

Chapter 6: Growth Mindset Matters | Alison Manoukian

Growing up, I was always a good student, earning good grades, and never failing a subject. In high school, I ranked in the top 20% of the state for English, Biology, Legal Studies, and Computing Studies. By the world's standards, I was a success. After school, I attended university and completed my Bachelor's with a double major in natural resource management and high school teaching.

I was a successful student, but I was still stuck. I asked myself, "How do I translate my success as a student and achieve in the real world? How can I succeed in a job, career, finances, and relationships?"

I never knew how to be anything other than a successful student. I have walked through financial hardship, anxiety, and depression. One day, I asked myself hard questions: "How did I get here? How will I fix it? Can I prosper? Can I be successful?" Have you found yourself at a similar crossroads in your own journey?

In high school, I overheard one of my teachers say that students who do well in school often don't succeed after leaving school. They don't transition well into the work environment. I remember thinking, "That will be me." I struggled with the idea of getting paid for what I did. I thought I had to be perfect and do everything exactly right.

When I finished university, my first full-time job was as a Landcare Coordinator. They wanted someone who cared about their programs. I realized that being a good student wouldn't "cut it" in the real world. I didn't have the technical skills, communication skills, or experience to do the job. I mentally broke down. I tried my hardest, but my hardest wasn't good enough. I no longer had confidence in my abilities. I began the difficult road from success at school to success at work and life. Sound familiar?

What made the transition from school to work so difficult for me, and what can you do to help your children transition successfully from school into real life, and work?

66

Growth Mindset

Mainstream education failed to teach me how to develop a growth mindset. It's not just what you do that makes you prosper and become successful, but what you think about work, your wellbeing, your past, and future— your purpose.

These were the missing ingredients I needed to grow up. Not intelligence, not good grades, not encouraging parents, not friends, not failure. I had a fixed mindset and low self-worth. I stood in the way of my own success. When I got out of my way, I saw myself as I truly was, seeing success and failure through a growth mindset. Things began to change.

A mindset is a belief you hold about your human qualities like intelligence, ability, talent and personality. It is what you think is true based on your thoughts and life experiences.

What do you think about intelligence? Can you become intelligent, or is intelligence determined at birth? Are talent and personality given to you at birth or do they develop over time based on your experiences? Do you have control over your personality, your intelligence or your talents? Your answers to these questions will help you discover whether you have a fixed or growth mindset.

Growth vs. Fixed Mindset

You have developed one of two mindsets: a growth mindset, or a fixed mindset. A growth mindset is the belief you can "grow" your intelligence, personality, talents and/or abilities over time, with effort and an effective system. A fixed mindset is the belief that your intelligence, talents, personality and abilities are fixed— that these traits cannot be changed, no matter how much effort you apply.

Growing up, I had a fixed mindset. My entire focus was not on learning, but on passing everything at school. My motivator was the fear of failure, not learning. I felt I needed to prove myself. In the work environment, this translated into reacting to any challenges with fear and a feeling of not being good enough to meet expectations— including my own and my perceived beliefs of the expectations of my managers and co-workers.

I believed that because I was getting paid, I wasn't allowed to make a mistake. I needed to be perfect. If I couldn't master a task immediately, I felt I wasn't good enough. I had a constant urge to quit (run away) to avoid these feelings of inferiority and failure.

You Can Change Your Mindset

Your brain is capable of change. You can build new connections and pathways in your brain to change the way you think. This ability of your brain to change can work for you or against you, depending on your choices, particularly what you choose to think, believe and focus on.

Science shows you can change your mindset, but change takes time, plus an active, directed effort. It takes 21 days to destroy your unhealthy mindset and 42 more days to grow your strong, healthy mindset.

Support your children to develop a growth mindset. Don't wait for the mainstream education system to do it. They steer children towards a fixed mindset through standardized testing, which only tests if your child knows what the government wants them to know. It is not an indication of intelligence. Don't only focus on test results. Help your child see the value of learning. Their worth is not based on performance, but on who they are. This sets them up for success now and in the future.

Now that you understand mindsets, what they are, and that you can alter them, take practical steps to build a growth mindset for yourself and your child.

Step 1: Re-Define "Failure"

When you hear the word "fail," do you see it as a negative or positive experience? For most, failure is a harmful, final judgment. It stirs up thoughts of not being good enough, failing to live up to the expectations of others, being "less than" and instills fear. At work, a fear of being fired. In school, fear what others think.

When you focus on the fear of failing, you focus on the outcome rather than the process. You avoid challenges not to prevent the activity but to avoid the chance of failure. You limit your ability to learn and grow— you are more likely to give up. However, you must realize that failure can be positive. Failure is, in fact, a *part* of success!

Look at failure through a growth mindset, and you won't see it as a final judgment of doom or a sign of lack, but your opportunity to learn. Failure shows you where we are now. Constructive feedback can provide you with a path forward from where you are, to where you want to be. Failure drives you to quit, but also drives you to succeed. To prosper in life, learn and grow from your failures. **Do not let them define or control you.**

Step 2: Focus on Strengths

The mainstream school system does children a great disservice, teaching them to focus on what they are not good at and what they don't enjoy.

What would you encourage your child to focus on if your child's report showed an A for physical education and a C for mathematics? Should your child focus on the C to improve mathematics? Or, concentrate on the A and build on their success in physical education? Would their teacher focus on their skill in physical education or on their need to improve in Mathematics?

When I worked as a tutor, I felt sad for the children, who attended school, spending a large part of their day on activities they hated, only to return home to spend another hour or two on more activities they hated, and felt they were not good at.

Returning to university for my Masters of Teaching, I had been away from school for ten years. I had to complete a Mathematics and English test to become a primary school teacher. I realized I had never used a vast majority of what I learned in mathematics in my life, career, or the real world. Yet, I spent countless hours studying mathematics at school. I found myself re-learning what I had forgotten through lack of use. The most successful people in this world are not good at everything. Instead, they have passion, something they do well, and focus on that.

Observe what your child does well, what they enjoy, and their strengths. Then link this back to their studies in Mathematics, English, Science, or other subjects. When focusing on their strengths, children are more engaged in the learning process— they feel good about themselves. Learning will have a purpose in propelling them towards their goals.

Step 3: Speak Growth

The words you use to talk to yourself and others, and the words they speak to you, make a big difference in how you think and believe. Phrases like "Clever Boy" when a child passes a test reinforces the idea that the outcome, not the performance, determines success, and supports the development of a fixed mindset— success is"clever" and failure is "dumb."

Instead, use phrases such as, "When you learn a new skill, it grows your brain." "The feeling that it is hard means you are learning." And, "What step can you take to get better at this?" This helps children to value their learning and develop a growth mindset that focuses on the process as well as the outcome.

Develop a growth mindset for you and your children to set you and them up for prosperity and success.

About Alison Manoukian

Alison Manoukian (nee Roy) was born in 1982 in Lithgow, New South Wales, Australia.

Alison truly believes that parents are a child's best teachers and has a passion for equipping and supporting parents who homeschool their children. She aims to provide quality, wholesome educational resources and training for homeschoolers in Australia and beyond.

Claim your complimentary discovery call at AlisonManoukian.com/discovery.

Chapter 7: Face Fear Head On to Become Unstoppable | Kerry McKenzie

As Jenny gripped the phone tightly, she felt her heart pounding in her chest. She tried to type the numbers on her smartphone. Her fingers fumbled. She started again. When someone answered, she stammered, but grew more confident as that person talked her through the process. Jenny knew this was a turning point in her life.

You will recognize the above symptoms of fear if you have been in a situation to experience them for yourself. It could have been a final school examination, a job interview, or appearing before a magistrate as you desperately try to stop your home from being repossessed. These situations are at the extreme ends of an anxiety producing event. They can happen in smaller ways throughout any day. The car that pulls out in front of you, or your child suddenly running ahead of you as you both cross the street.

Fear

Maybe it is as silly as thinking there is someone in your room as you wake up suddenly at night, only to realize it is your dressing gown hanging on the door. As relief floods through your body, you feel your heartbeat slowing and your breathing return to normal. You may have begun to sweat before realizing there was no threat. Your body's response to fear is universal. It is programmed to protect you by retreating or preparing to fight that situation that creates the threat.

What made Jenny so fearful of making that call? She was making an appointment to finally stop smoking, which came with a guarantee.

Fear lies to you. Don't listen to it. Instead, find a trusted person to confide in, and listen to *them*. Fear is expensive, quite literally, from a smoking perspective.

Fear is a "giant" that you must overcome to succeed. It will hold you back if you do nothing to overcome it.

How did fear create that situation where Jenny was afraid of making a call to stop smoking? She listened to "that voice" in her own head.

Can you relate to the following? (Translate your own circumstances if smoking is not your issue.)

- What makes you think you can quit smoking?
- You tried so many times before, and look how they turned out!
- You just get cranky with everyone and cannot concentrate. You will gain weight again. You always do when you stop smoking.
- Will I be able to deal with the cravings? Everyone talks about how bad they are. I only lasted a week last time.
- Will I envy other people who continue to smoke? Will I want to join them outside during my break times? Will I be able to be near smokers and not want to have one myself?
- What do I do with my hands when I am working on a project? I am used to always being able to have a cigarette when I want, and it helps me concentrate.

Does any of this sound familiar? You can be your own worst enemy if you listen to your fears.

For the smoker, perhaps there is a fear of illness, or death, if the illness is already apparent. This is outweighed in a smoker's mind by other fears. **Your**

subconscious mind can create many ways to keep you where you are.

The Deeper Issue

Added to these thoughts are doubts about hypnotherapy in general, and as a stop smoking process specifically. Will it work? Will I be in control? Will he/she make me cluck like a chicken? (This is a common fear, believe it or not.)

What was really at the bottom of Jenny's thoughts? On the surface, it can look like a fear of failure, reinforced by the times she tried to stop smoking in the past. This backs up with a lack of self-esteem about her interpretation of her mood changes, cravings and weight gain on each of her previous attempts.

What is behind most smokers' fears of quitting cigarettes? "Who am I without a cigarette in my hand? In other words, will I even recognize myself?"

This may seem absurd to a non- smoker, but someone who has smoked for a few years will recognize the pattern.

- You have a stressful situation at work. Your solution: go outside for a cigarette. You need "fresh air" anyway, and it gives you some space from the problem.
- The kids are getting you down: Get them occupied with something (it does not matter what it is) while you duck outside for a cigarette.
- An argument with a partner: Same solution, but without the hassle of finding them something to do for the time you will be outside.
- You get a promotion at work: time to celebrate, which will always include a cigarette alongside the drink.
- A birthday, anniversary, special night out, a graduation, wedding, or any other cause for a celebration: For most smokers, these are also a time to have a cigarette.

Examine these possible fears. Smoking takes up a large part of a smoker's life. The time spent smoking can equal a part time job, but this is a part time job Jenny and others pay for in their time and money.

If nothing else was to be gained, a substantial increase in time each day would be a positive outcome. Some people say they feel a sense of great freedom once they stop smoking, as if a great weight has been lifted.

What About Your Fears?

Maybe you do not smoke but have something else in your life you keep putting off. Would making that change cause you to feel a great weight lifted from your shoulders?

You may want to make a major decision involving a change in your employment. You have security in a regular wage and accumulated benefits. You may enjoy your work, but work culture does not sit well with you. Perhaps the next step out of the known is frightening, and not just for the financial possibilities.

Are you contemplating whether you should move from your current house? What is holding you back from doing it? Have you had your house valued, or checked properties in the area you would like to move to? If not, why not? Is it just a dream, or are those voices of fear keeping you where you are?

Are you concerned over pandemic restrictions placed on you? Perhaps you are fearful of the possible negative health outcomes for you and your family? Maybe you are in one of the above-mentioned situations due to the continual lockdowns and change in employment. These are real scenarios for many people. The difference in your outcome will be in the way you master your fear of the unknown.

How did Jenny manage her fear of the unknown? In her case, the fear had many aspects. She had failed in her previous attempts to quit cigarettes, so a fear of repeated failure was a concern.

Jenny stopped listening to the inner voices which had controlled her to that point. While still nervous at the thought of the phone call, and the commitment she was about to make, she carried it through.

Being afraid to take the first step is no reason not to take it.

The Solution is a Mentor

Perhaps Jenny also had a mentor she trusted to talk through her plans before the call. If she did not have that person in her life, she had a mentor in her hypnotherapist to guide her through the process and follow up to ensure her lifelong success.

Stop listening to the fear. Speak with someone you trust, who is outside the situation. You need a mentor to get through this scary change. Having someone with a different point of view can make it clearer. You will wonder why you did not see the solution. You were tied up in the negative emotions and had been "going over it" for so long that a new path could not appear. An outsider views it without the emotional attachment binding you to your fear.

Take Action Now

Ask someone else to sit by your side and help you through this new and scary time in your life. It can be a friend you trust to help you navigate the situation.

For big changes, such as real estate moves and financial situations, consult an expert. Do not ask your neighbor for their advice. Would you ask your plumber for advice on your toothache, or your dentist about your blocked drain? Of course not, but it's easy to take well-intentioned but misinformed advice from "comfortable" family and friends.

Get out of your comfort zone. "Being comfortable" is another way to avoid facing up to the rut your fears have placed you in over time. For the smoker, this means not being able to see who they can be without cigarettes, even if they want to quit. If you put off the move to another job, starting your own business, or physically moving house, you remain in your comfort zone. You allow your fear of a new situation to rule your life. Your fight or flight response remains firmly in retreat mode, as you seek to avoid conflict.

How did Jenny fare once she had made that first (scary) call? She spoke with the hypnotherapist who asked pertinent questions and then an appointment in two weeks. It gave Jenny time to become sure of her decision and to make plans for her new life.

Jenny had a mentor qualified to help her situation. Once she attended her appointment, Jenny found the process relaxing and walked out feeling free of the old habit. The changes she and her therapist had planned for her first thirty days were written down, and she prepared a different space at home for relaxation times. This broke the old associations with smoking.

She knew that if she fell back in the future, she could call for a follow up session. With careful planning with her mentor this was unlikely to be needed, but it was reassuring that it was there. Jenny knew that this time she was successful. She felt unstoppable and looked forward to other changes in her life. The financial and health benefits were obvious but the other freedoms she found made that first phone call one of the best moves in her life.

What is stopping you from making yourself unstoppable?

- What changes do you want to make?
- Who do you need as your mentor to make it happen?
- What is your scary moment for that initial phone call?

Begin by writing answers to these questions. I know it can be daunting, but the first step is usually the hardest.

Don't let your fear of the unknown be the disability that stops you reaching your true potential. I wish you success in the area of your life you wish to change.

About Kerry McKenzie

Kerry McKenzie has an extensive background as a Registered Nurse and educator which has led to a career teaching in many aspects of health and well-being. This has included students in  varied situations from university courses to aged care and community settings.

Kerry was drawn to studies in NLP, including master practitioner and trainer levels. Her previous qualifications and experience in health and educational counseling these areas come together to assist clients on their way to making their own changes to improve health outcomes. Her website is: KerryMcKenzieOnline.com.

Chapter 8: Grow Up to Become the Best Version of Yourself | PJ Ashley

It's about time for you to become the creator in your own life. If not now, when?

Too many people spend their lives "waiting" to be happy, healthy, and wealthy— living a life of purpose and joy.

Your future is an illusion and your past is a memory. Every point in your journey is a creation manifested from your past, in your past, experienced now. Everything you choose can be within the grasp of your understanding, here and now.

As a child, you experienced life in the present, not fearing the future, but living day to day. Whether or not your childhood was wonderful, filled with love, joy and excitement, or whether your childhood was filled with fear, dread, and lack, you were concerned about your presence, immediate needs and desires.

As you age and experience life, you pick up the knowledge of mistakes, needs not met, desires not fulfilled, and wants not realized— creating stress, doubt and an elongated timeline.

Escape Your Timeline

When you are truly in the present, focused, there is nothing that you truly desire. There may be choices you would like to create, and manifestations you would like to materialize into action, but when you are truly present, there is no need.

The greater the stress you place on yourself and your life, your expectations, and your requirement to fulfill other people's expectations of you, the greater your mind creates the timeline.

When you have a negative perception of your past that causes you grief, sadness and loss of energy... you create a great perception over a negative future with fear, doubt and anxiety. You avoid the present.

If you experience depression or anxiety, you *live through a timeline* of life rather than *experiencing* the presence of life.

You will experience events that sadden you into depression (from the past) and fears that manifest as anxiety (in the future). The key to living peacefully is managing this, being aware of this, and being the master of your timeline— being the creator in your life's journey.

Manifestation

To be your own creator, you must develop the skills to be present. Do you know how to manifest? Can you create with your highest consciousness, your greatest connection, and know how to be the master conductor (controller) of your choosing?

Adults constantly ask children, "When you grow up, what will you be?" The child will usually respond with an experience they know— copying their parents career, or an activity they had recently witnessed.

Each time that question is asked, children can change their response dependent upon their most recent experiences, as children are more interested in what is happening NOW, eating NOW, playing NOW, the conversation with their parents NOW, the attention they are seeking NOW for the fulfilment of their immediate desires. And they are master manipulators to make sure they receive it .

Children live in the present— choosing, selecting, desiring for the present, not caring very much about the past, not wishing about their future. It is a fun, and free life when supported by loving parents or adults. Why did you lose this ability as an adult? More importantly, how do you get it back?

To be the creator in your own world is to connect to your highest consciousness, love, light oneness, God, or whatever name you are comfortable calling it. Know, accept and be excited that you are the creator in your own world.

Next Opportunity Waiting

As children live in the now, you can also bring your past back into your present positive control. Minimize your timeline down to something within your positive memories and expectations. Access one of the universal laws of creation.

NOW, an acronym for "Next Opportunity Waiting"— allows you to be present, knowing that you are in control of the growth of your life. Being present not only *does not* limit your ability to create magnificent happiness, health and wealth with purpose and fun for your future, but it is imperative that you are present to do these things.

"I'll be happy when..." places you in present lack, and therefore, future lack. "I will do something about my health when..." places you in a current disorder or dysfunction in present health, and therefore lack of health in the future. "I will feel wealthy when..." places you in present financial lack, and therefore lacking a financially free future.

"There is no purpose or reasonable meaning to my life now" creates a meaningless future. "There is no joy, no opportunity for joy, money for joy etc", is a joyless present and creates a joyless future.

Not being on your present timeline can create a depressed feeling from the past and anxiety of the future. The present is also the point of creation. What has been stopping you, blocking you, sabotaging you, from being calm, in control and confident today? Being the master of your journey?

Once you know this, you will stop sabotaging your journey, the magnificence of being present and therefore you will stop sabotaging the creation of the future in its most positive and magical form.

Look at the question: when I grow up I'd like to be? When I...

- G - gratefully
- R - request
- O - opportunities
- W - wisely
- U - universally, &
- P - presently

I'd like to be?

Happy, Healthy, Wealthy: Living a Life of Purpose and Joy

What are you missing from your present? What would you like, or love, to have in your future? What has purpose? What brings you joy? Consider the three answers that come to mind, and immediately write these three things down.

Look at the first answer you wrote down. Analyze it to determine if it maps to the GROW UP acronym. Are you:

- **Gratefully:** Are you Grateful for everything that has lead you to this choice now, in the present?
- **Request:** Have you Requested this to appear in your present?
- **Opportunities:** Do you believe this is an Opportunity you deserve to create and have?
- **Wisely:** Is it a wise choice?
- **Universally:** Is it a universal choice? Is it more than just your mind? More than just a physical desire? Holistically, through a choice that embodies the entirety of you, the oneness of you, the collective consciousness of your mind, body and soul?

- **Presently:** Have you chosen this in the present? FEEL this into your creation while you're in the NOW. In the total awareness and energy of your heart, the hub of your creation.

If the answer is yes, continue with your other two choices. FEEL into them and see if they meet the requirement of the "When I GROW UP" statement.

If your three choices do not meet the requirement of When I GROW UP, go back into your NOW, into your presence, into your next opportunity waiting.

The World is Waiting For You

There are many ways to bring you into that presence and out of that monkey mind, out of your physical pain, out of your lack, doubt, fear.

One of them is focusing on your breath. Be mindful of the present situation, reading each word on the page, stopping to focus on one image, shutting out all distractions, and bring yourself back into "now." FEELING, experiencing, knowing that you are part of the oneness, the collective consciousness of all mankind, and just as deserving to be with receiving as anyone else on the planet.

One of my all-time favorite quotes is, "The best thing you can do for the poor, is not be one yourself." It gave me permission to love with all my heart, be spiritually connected, and be at peace with my value and financial rewards. Do not be poor in happiness, nor health, nor wealth, nor purpose, nor joy. Acknowledge that you are a part of the conscious creation of the world, and therefore a part of, and not separate to, creation.

Accept that you can change your happiness in the present. Your ill health is a creation from your past. Your future life is a manifestation of what you create now. These are the important keys to stop your stressed, depressed or anxious state. You can be in control of your own destiny.

Journey of Yours

Creation is fun when it has purpose and joy. JOY, the acronym for "Journey Of Yours," is your path, your purpose, and your direction. If your life does not have joy currently, then you are not on your path, your purpose, or in your direction.

Regardless if you have spiritual, religious or agnostic beliefs, most people have an understanding that you have come into this life to experience a life of meaning, in a world that has opportunities to present you with joy and purpose. When you can see, sense, know, and feel that, you'll see that your life has purpose and meaning. However, your purpose cannot come from lack, doubt, nor fear, but from fully understanding that you create the most conscious, connected and confident life you can choose.

You have skills, abilities and gifts that are a part of your creation and a part of your world. It is time for you to step up into that, GROW UP into that, lift up into that, and become the best version of yourself that you can be. A self that is happy, healthy, and wealthy, with purpose and joy. This is not a rehearsal, this is *the journey of yours.*

Humanity is at a turning point on its journey, with truth, change and growth giving you an amazing opportunity to become the best version of yourself.

Create happiness, health, and wealth, and see your purpose. Discover your reason for being, and why, and how this is linked to your joy. Find your peace and you find your joy. Find your joy and you find your journey. Find your journey and you find your purpose. Find your purpose and you find your wealth. Find your wealth and you find your health. Find your health and you find your happiness. This is the creation of life.

What are you choosing to create? What will you do when you GROW UP?

It's about time to become the creator in your own life and fast forward to your success NOW. If not now, when? The world is waiting.

About PJ Ashley

Everyone deserves the chance to heal and experience the most out of life and business. PJ is helping and training others as the Founder and CEO of The Pillar Code.

The Pillar Code is "a unique journey of healing" that connects people and businesses to happiness, health and wealth improvements through Life, Mind, Body and Business transformation, with spectacular results.

Join The Creator's Club Community at ThePillarCode.com. Filled with tools, techniques, personal messages, workshops, inspiration, and momentum to fast forward to success. Receive a FREE month with Promo Code: TCClubPJ.

Chapter 9: Paws Are Yours for Life | Robin Oliver

Ask me how much I love animals, and I will tell you that I was *always* in love with animals from an early age— especially dogs!

I always had a soft spot for an animal that looked at me with soft loving eyes, making me think, "You are beautiful! Would my mother notice if I brought you home? I could hide you in my bedroom!"

Like all children, I thought, if I kept asking my mother constantly, she would let me have a dog of my own.

My first dog was a Cocker Spaniel, who, thankfully, had a very soft nature. I loved him.

When I was first married, we bought a Labrador puppy. In hindsight, this was not the best idea. We both worked full time. This lonely puppy, without guidance from us during the day, got into mischief. This puppy had no learning boundaries during our working hours. Dogs are pack animals: they need constant support and guidance during this formative learning time.

An Opportunity Presents Itself

I waited for a more opportune time to bring dogs back into my life. This opportunity came about when I was home as a mother raising our two young boys.

I desperately wanted a dog I could show in the showroom to achieve its Australian championship. My father-in-law said, "You will never achieve that!" He did not want me to be disappointed if I could not achieve this goal.

This raised an immediate determined and inward response from me: "Do not count on that. I will show you that I can do it."

I purchased a pedigree Maltese dog and showed her to her Australian Championship Title. At first, I wasn't very skilled, but I put my heart and soul into learning how to train her, groom, and teach her.

After being in a business for a few years, I desperately wanted to return to the dog world. I decided to trial my dogs in obedience and agility.

Daily Guidance

I chose Shelties, having a small backyard. Being involved in business with another family, I was able to take my first Sheltie to work with me. I knew from past experience this puppy needed my daily guidance. This presented a perfect opportunity for me to be hands-on raising this puppy each day. This puppy had a wonderful life, traveled to work with me, met lots of people, and was socialized. I taught him the behavior I expected. He became a loved member of our household.

This puppy was a barker. I was previously not used to this issue with my Maltese Dogs.

I had let the barking issue continue for too long. I determined that any new puppy or dog in our household would need to understand boundaries to become a welcome addition to our family.

My next Sheltie was a gorgeous 10 week old puppy. The breeder was reluctant to part with her. I watched the breeder cry about this puppy, and I thought, I cannot beg for this puppy.

Thankfully, the breeder let me leave with this delightful and happy puppy. I joyously took her home, knowing that I was going to carefully monitor this puppy from the start, with love and consistency.

Planning, Routine, Repetition & Encouragement

Arriving home, this gorgeous sparkling puppy met my other dog (the barker) who immediately became jealous and wanted no part of her.

I needed to make them friends and establish a daily routine we all understood. My first task was to keep her close to me so she would feel safe and secure. I had the puppy on a lead, and/or used a door barrier in a room I was working in, keeping the puppy close to me— being mindful that a new puppy must be taken outside every 30 to 60 minutes to the toilet.

I took the puppy outside to the toilet, on a lead, with my "command" being, "toilet!" Once she obliged, I offered a treat and praised her profusely, saying, "Good girl"— and adding, "What a clever dog."

With a puppy or rehomed dog, this must be the same process each time, so she understands this is what I expect of her in our household. Some dogs catch on to this quickly, but it might require more patience. It doesn't matter how long it takes, as long as it is the same consistent process.

A new puppy must go outside to the toilet as soon as they wake up, have a meal, a drink, or quick play.

All animal age groups need encouragement in this new environment— they feel unsure of themselves.

Once this pattern becomes part of the animal's routine, I only have to say the chosen verbal command, and she obliges willingly, especially if the reward is coming back inside or going for a walk. This verbal command is helpful when taking her to an outing or new environment. It reduces stress when the dog can toilet on command.

She obliges willingly because I consistently take her out each time on her lead to relieve herself, then reward her. I do this through the night. Even when it is raining, we go outside, umbrella in hand, to protect us from the elements, and "voila"... all finished.

I train my dogs to be happy in a crate. Many incorrectly think this is harmful to the dog. Not so! In packs, dogs dig out a tunnel (lair) to curl up in from danger and the elements.

I get down on the floor with the dog to be at her level, and I open the crate door, having ready yummy treats to throw in. I encourage the dog to happily enter and eat the treat. Then, I call the dog back out for another treat from me, repeating again and again, throwing the treat in, calling back out for a treat from me, making this a happy and fun time for the dog. Every time you think of this, get on the floor and repeat.

Gradual Progress

The dog now understands that coming back out from the crate is a reward. For a few nights, I place her in the crate, in my bedroom, to sleep for the night so she knows company is nearby. If she wakes through the night, I take her out on a lead to relieve herself. She soon responds to this routine.

Once I am confident my new family addition can go through the night without me waking up, I put her in the room I choose within my house to sleep each night.

She learns to love her crate. This is especially handy when you have visitors— your dog can safely and happily lie in her crate.

I expect my animal to be calm when needed. A new puppy, or even an older rehomed dog, may take a long while to respond to being calm.

When I notice my puppy becoming over excited, I call her to my side and massage the sides of her body. I pat her with long strokes until she calms down. Next, I reward her, and repeat this process, long deliberate pats, treating until she relaxes.

The "Learning to Be Calm" Phase

If my puppy is too excited and is not in a relaxing frame of mind, I put her back in her crate to chill. I do not scold— she needs to learn this is a quiet time. I normally have a pen setup outside. The dog can take time out to calm down, or have a nap, and know that I am not far away.

This phase, learning to be calm, can take weeks or months. Patience and consistency from the human leader is the key to success.

Another important milestone: the dog must look me in the eye for direction, or look lovingly with great respect. I must earn my puppy's respect, and she will earn my respect.

Sheepdogs work away from their master. When in the close-to-medium range, my puppy looks to my eyes for direction, watchful for hand signals. She needs to be trained to learn verbal commands. Even at a great distance, she looks back to me for direction. Sheepdogs need this skill to lead the sheep. Watching these great working animals is a lesson in teamwork. The bond a dog develops with her master is close, rewarding, and a learned skill that takes time to implement.

Learning This Skill Was Not As Easy As I Expected

During a routine check at my vet with my latest puppy, an Australian Kelpie, 10 weeks of age, my vet asked me how confident I was in having my dog keep eye contact with me. This was not an issue— I had taught my Shelties to look at me through clicker and treat training. Clicker training is a valuable tool to learn, known as "shaping your dog."

My vet chuckled, saying, "Kelpies are much different than Shelties. Let me show you how I do it!" He picked up my squirming puppy, turned her gently onto her back on the vet table, and scratched her tummy. Do you think this squirming puppy gave him eye contact? No! She turned her head from side to side, and did not want to accept this person needed her to look directly. Eventually, her eyes made contact with his. Much to her surprise, this brought praise from this human.

I'm sure she thought, "Oops, I didn't mean to do that!" She looked from side to side, avoiding eye contact. When she finally made eye contact again, she was rewarded for doing so. After five minutes, she made eye contact more easily. My vet said, "Now it's your turn..."

Be Persistent & Patient

It took me longer than five minutes to connect with her eyes. My vet smiled. He said, "Do not be offended. Your puppy recognizes that I am male and you are female. I am not showing disrespect. It is just what an animal recognizes."

107

When I arrived home, I placed my dog on her back on my lap. When she was on the floor playing with me and was prepared to allow me to scratch her tummy, we practiced eye contact. It took 24 hours before this new Kelpie puppy made eye contact without feeling she had given away her closely guarded independence. Each time she made eye contact, we had a praise party. What fun we shared!

Do not be discouraged if it takes two weeks or longer to achieve eye contact. If this is a dog you are re-homing, you do not know how this dog has been treated previously. They may need special care to feel confident and secure in your company.

Your dog's comfort levels are paramount. I work on this exercise with patience until we have success. This is an important process to get your dog to show great respect for you. People are amazed at how well behaved my dogs are. I'm confidently invited back for more visits with my precious companions.

About Robin Oliver

Robin Oliver has always considered animals to be special, especially dogs. Our lives are enriched by sharing time with these precious animals that become our pets.

Robin has bred pedigree Maltese dogs for years and some have attained their Australian Championship titles, won Group awards and a Best in Show award.

Your dogs are such wonderful and valued companions. Free of charge, watch her three-part video series, showing you the results of the training you need to apply when you introduce a new puppy or dog to your household. Watch it at: RobinOliverOnline.com.

Chapter 10: My Health Journey Begins | Vicki Stanford

I was sitting in a business meeting with girls from our skin care company. All of a sudden, a strange feeling came over me. A dizziness! An electric shock! A wave of nausea, traveling through my head, my heart and through my whole body. I knew something was very wrong. The chatter of the girls faded into the distance. I pulled out my mobile phone and checked that I had the ambulance number handy.

My adult daughter sat on my left. Not wanting to alarm her, I made sure she couldn't see my phone. On my right was Annette, a good friend and a personal trainer.

"Annette," I said quietly. "I feel weird right now. I just want to let someone know. Something's wrong."

She discreetly took my wrist and checked my pulse.

"You seem okay," she said. "That's normal. What else do you feel?"

I did my best to describe the symptoms without disturbing the meeting. The other girls continued to discuss the latest skin care specials and package deals.

It passed, to a degree, but I still felt very strange. Thankfully, my daughter was driving, because I didn't feel safe to drive.

Just One of Those Things?

When I arrived home, I called my doctor and booked an appointment for the next day, before going to lie down. The doctor called it "just one of those things" — not the most enlightening diagnosis, but I was grateful he couldn't find anything wrong. Blood pressure, normal. Heart rate, normal. Still it left a nagging doubt. Did I imagine it? Was I just over-stressed? Was I losing the plot?

By the end of the week, I had come down with the flu. I had never been happier to catch the flu. That's what it was all about! I spent three days in bed and another few days regaining my strength, grateful to put it behind me. The night before I was due to go back to work, I had a slightly strange sensation again. *Not happening!* I thought to myself. *I imagined that. I'm just being paranoid.* I got off the couch and went to bed early.

The next day I was taking a client to an appointment. We were on our way there when the dizziness returned. This time I was driving. My mind raced. Do I tell him? We were nearly there and I didn't want to alarm him. I slowed down and drove in the left lane.

"Where is this place?" I asked casually. I knew exactly where it was but I was scouting ahead for pullover places, just in case. We arrived and I pulled into the carpark. I noticed a medical clinic on the other side of the road.

"You've got this," I said to my client. "We've been over it and over it. You don't need me to come in. Just tell it from the heart."

While he was in the appointment, I quickly crossed over to the medical clinic, explained my situation and asked if anyone could see me at really short notice. Thankfully, they could. Once again: blood pressure, heart rate. This time, they also tested my blood sugars. All normal. After a glass of water and paying the bill, I managed to get back across the road before my client was finished. Maybe I was just dehydrated!

"How did it go?" I smiled, as he entered the waiting room, hoping it looked genuine.

We discussed his project on the way back and I was able to forget my symptoms for a while.

Wouldn't It Be Better to Find Out the Cause?

That night, I poured out my woes to my husband. Was this what anxiety felt like? I had always dismissed anxious people as "worry warts" who needed to learn to take a deep breath. Thankfully, the next day was a day off so I decided to rest.

Over the next few weeks, I asked my husband to take me to our local emergency department at least twice. It kept happening. They performed ECGs and took blood samples. At least I knew I wasn't having a heart attack! They sent me home with tablets to stop the dizziness.

"But what is causing the dizziness?" I asked. "Wouldn't it be better to find out the cause than to just mask the symptoms?"

No-one was nearly as interested in this idea as I was. I discovered that mainstream medicine (and my doctor) just doesn't have the time and resources to sit and discuss all the possibilities. But they will send you to expensive specialists.

The heart clinic was quite an eye-opener. During the stress test — on the treadmill — I had the distinct impression that they were worried I might collapse. I was disappointed when they stopped the test well below my maximum capacity. I was ready to show them what this 50-something-year-old grandmother could do. I hadn't spent all those hours in the gym for nothing! The ultrasound on my heart was fascinating as I watched them measure the size of my heart on the screen. I was sent home, wired up with a monitor to wear over the weekend. Again, all this came to nothing as far as a diagnosis was concerned. (Definitely not a "nothing" when it came to the cost.) On my follow up visit, the heart specialist cheerfully announced that the next step was to have surgery to insert a monitor under the skin — permanently. *Wait! What?* I thought.

"But you've found nothing wrong," I said.

"No," he replied. "But if there is anything we haven't picked up, it will show eventually."

"Are there side effects with an electrical device next to my heart? Can it interfere?" I asked, my concern growing.

"Side effects are rare, but if that happens, we can put in a pacemaker," he replied. I couldn't get out of there fast enough!

Choices to Make

I was starting to discover that specialists are very focused on their own areas and don't look at the body as a whole. My concern was that this would lead to a downward spiral of treating side-effects caused by the previous specialist's treatment.

It seemed I had some choices to make. Do I turn my body over to medical science while I'm still alive? Or do I do my own research and take responsibility for my own health?

So I started researching! I read everything I could get my hands on. Seminars. Supplements. Finding medical professionals who looked at the body as a whole and understood that every system affects the others. I started to get a feel for who to follow. This information was not readily available through "Dr Google" but as I read material, or followed one expert, I found referrals to others. I noticed common threads which helped me navigate through the material and discern good and bad information. It showed me the next step in my personal journey.

"You Are What You Eat" is Only Partly True

I consulted a naturopath. She did a live blood test. I was so fascinated to see my blood cells on the screen. They didn't look quite as I had expected. More like gear cogs than nice circles.

"Are they supposed to look like that?" I asked.

"No. They should be round and smooth," she replied. "Plus, they should be moving freely and not in clumps."

She suggested mineral supplements. I had been taking vitamins for some time, so I was surprised that I was deficient. I learned that minerals are even more important than vitamins. Food has become mineral deficient due to modern farming practices. In some circumstances, our bodies can produce their own vitamins — but not minerals. They are the primary building blocks that must come from the environment. Also, many vitamin supplements are synthetic and your body can't absorb them. "You are what you eat" is only true if you are absorbing and assimilating the good stuff: all the way to your cells.

One of, if not the, most important of those minerals is magnesium. I was magnesium deficient, and probably so are you. We all are, but it doesn't show on blood tests because your body carefully controls the amount of magnesium in the blood to keep you alive. The problem: it is very challenging to get enough magnesium into our cells where it is essential for literally hundreds of functions. It is difficult to absorb through our gut, even with the most absorbable types. I had to learn to find other ways to get it into my cells.

As the live blood examination continued, she pointed out many fascinating things, just doing their job under the microscope, as if they were still surging through my veins. There were fat cells. She used big words like leukocytes, platelets and macrophages — the "Pac-Men" inside you.

"There's a candida cell," she casually mentioned. My curiosity changed to alert.

"In my blood?" I said, stating the obvious. I didn't think that was supposed to be there. I knew candida was unhealthy yeast that caused all sorts of nasty skin symptoms. What was it doing in my blood? It turns out that systemic candida (through your whole system) is connected with "leaky gut" and leads to allergies, autoimmune diseases, irritable gut syndrome and a host of other illnesses.

Over 2,000 years ago, Hippocrates wrote, "All disease begins in the gut." It seems that mainstream medicine has only begun to understand this in the last 20 years.

I Was Sick Long Before I Knew It

My "hitting the wall" experience was my wake-up call: but I had warning signs a long time beforehand — I just didn't recognize them. My sickness journey began decades earlier.

As a teenager I was put on antibiotics for severe acne. No-one understood, back then, the damage antibiotics does to our gut and our good gut bacteria — known as our microbiome. The microbiome is like an internal garden. We need a wide variety of good bacteria, and also a few bad ones, to be in perfect balance to have great health. Like any garden, if you "nuke" all the plants and end up with bare ground, what will grow back, all by themselves? The weeds! Likewise, if you kill off the good bacteria in your gut, it allows an overgrowth of bad bacteria and yeasts like candida.

Another early warning sign that I missed was depression. We were training at work to recognize the signs of depression in others, so we did the questionnaire ourselves. I had never considered myself to be depressed. I thought my experience was normal. Perhaps I was emotional and unmotivated, but I thought I had a positive view of life. I just blamed the challenges of being a busy Mum.

My score was bad and sad. (Pun intended.) In hindsight, I should have taken heed of those test results as early signs of a later problem.

A Winding Road of Discovery

Around the time of the strange symptoms, we had some holidays, so we headed off on a road trip through northern South Australia and into western New South Wales and Queensland. I was quite nervous about going. What if I have another "episode" while we are literally out the back of Bourke. (An Australian outback town.)

First major stop was at Broken Hill. What a beautiful and interesting old town. We needed a couple of nights to see the sights and visit the art galleries. As the trip progressed I started to relax and feel a lot better. We were driving off into the Aussie outback and life was good. I started to feel normal again and came out of my high alert mindset.

A few days into the trip, I was enjoying the scenery as my husband drove. He pulled out to pass the car in front. I could see a car coming towards us from the other direction. He overtook and pulled back in safely.

"Do you think you cut that a bit fine?" I asked.

"No. I had a good view ahead," he replied. I agreed.

My head told me that his judgment was sound and he was driving safely. My body, on the other hand, went into a panic reaction. I broke into a sweat and my hands were shaking. I did some deep breathing to calm my reaction: all the while observing myself like a third person.

I'll file this away for my naturopath and try to enjoy my holiday, I thought.

We continued through the Murray Darling Basin: Through cotton country and mining areas. We didn't plan too far ahead, just phoning for a room each night, once we knew how far we would get. We had no set plan, except to be in Townsville to see friends by the end of the third week. Some places were so lovely we stayed an extra night. Some were pretty bad and we moved on quickly. We just let the road lead us. Toward the end of our trip, when I had really unwound and almost forgotten about my medical issues, we happened upon a health expo. There was a stall from a new company specializing in magnesium! Not tablets, but oils and creams to absorb through the skin. I had the privilege of talking to them for a long time and taking home some product and lots of reading material.

That trip was a metaphor for my health journey: A winding road of discovery. Don't plan too far ahead, just learn from what is happening right now — then move to the next thing when you are ready. My ultimate destination was clear — optimal health — but it would take a journey to get there. Our bodies are designed as self-healing organisms. Believe in your body's innate ability to heal itself, with a little help from your friends!

I'm grateful to the people who have contributed to my healing journey. I recently sat in the office of one of those special people, who announced my blood results were "perfect." I have come full circle. Unfortunately, the world is as toxic as ever, and we have to work even harder at looking after our health. It's one of the most important things you can do!

About Vicki Stanford

Vicki Stanford is a wife, mother and grandmother who lives in the beautiful Adelaide Hills in South Australia. She is passionate about helping other women navigate life, health and family. Vicki has been studying natural health for more than 10 years through her own health journey. She believes in the body's God-given ability to heal itself — when given the right environment. In her spare time Vicki likes to sing, to write and grow her edible garden — or just to spend time with people!

Please use this link for a free mini-series that will inspire you to begin your own optimum health journey: VickiStanford.com/freeoffer.

Chapter 11: Fast Forward to the Results You Deserve and Live Your Best Life Ever | David Cavanagh

Like all good stories, this one starts, "Once Upon A Time..."

Once upon a time, there was a guy named David Cavanagh who had no money, was a single father of a beautiful daughter named Krystal, who was told by everyone how smart and awesome he was, yet he could barely pay his rent each week.

So much for being "smart and awesome!"

David had to be the life of every party he attended. He was the "comedian and joker" everyone had to have around, but the "inside" of David was definitely not what he was portraying on the "outside." He was

125

actually the joke of the party and not just the one telling the jokes.

David was a very lonely man who was crying out to be loved, to be wanted, to be noticed, to be listened to, and he did everything just to be the center of attention.

This attention fed David's ego and low self-esteem to the level where it put a smile on his face. It kept him feeling "okay to be alive."

David was living in Mudgeeraba on the Gold Coast in Queensland, Australia and his only form of income was receiving a single parent's pension each fortnight to help him, and his daughter Krystal survive from day to day.

He was renting a 3-bedroom townhouse with a guy named Dennis Hall and he could barely pay Dennis his half of the rent each week. Life was definitely not pleasant for David Cavanagh. In fact, it was living hell at the time.

"The" Phone Call

Then one day while David was at home laying on his couch, he got a phone call. The phone call was from Adam Hudson who was the co-founder of a company called the "Better Business Institute."

This company was actually run by Peter Sun and Adam Hudson— two very successful and talented marketers, entrepreneurs and businessmen who had kicked several home runs in many of their previous businesses.

Picture this— David was sitting at home and got Adam's phone call at 7:52PM in the evening when he was usually sitting down relaxing watching TV.

The phone conversation went something like this: "Hi David, it's Adam. Peter Sun and I are looking for someone to help with our in-house Internet Marketing and when we sat down and brainstormed, the name which kept coming into our heads was David Cavanagh. Do you mind coming in for an interview with Peter and I tomorrow morning?"

Of course, David said "Yes" and the following day David went in to see Adam and Peter.

Now I'll recall everything as it happened looking back in hindsight:

When I was being interviewed back then, Adam told me how I was a really talented guy. He said I was an immensely talented guy when it came to copywriting, sales, motivation, personal development, persuasion, internet marketing, and SEO.

I felt so good when Adam complimented me because it filled my low self-esteem bucket and made me feel wanted, noticed, accepted, and loved at the time.

I thought, "I can't believe I'm hearing all these great comments about me." Then Adam dropped the bombshell on our great conversation:

"David, we feel you're focusing your energy 1% on 100 things, rather than putting 100% energy and focus onto one thing. If Peter and I are to employ you, you need to stop this immediately and start doing everything the way we ask you or you won't have a job."

This was the part of the conversation which really got up my nose.

Intense Focus

I didn't know whether to take Adam's comments as a huge insult, or to shut my mouth and put my pride and ego to the side and simply keep listening to him. I mean, what was I supposed to think at the time?

After all, he'd invited me in for an interview, so he must have felt I was definitely worth talking to in the first place. Why was I doubting myself?

Have you ever had the feeling of being down in the dumps, yet not knowing where to go or what to do with your life? That's what I felt like at that moment.

The feeling of not knowing who to turn to for help. The lack of thoughts of not knowing what direction you should be taking each and every day.

I was great at helping other people get massive results. This was me back then. This was a totally different David Cavanagh to the David Cavanagh nowadays. Now here are some huge takeaways for you:

I could have stayed the same. I could have kept talking rubbish to myself. I could have kept going on and on with the never-ending thoughts of how good I was, how I was better than everyone else, how I knew everything about anything (even though I was struggling to pay my bills, struggling to put food in my mouth each week and the ongoing hassles of keeping the debt collectors away from my front door).

I really needed to change my life, and Adam's words were the catalyst for me to start changing immediately. It was up to me to change. Change comes from within.

Follow One Course Until Successful

Three months after working with Adam and Peter, I was told by the team in the office how they were all flying down from the Gold Coast to Sydney to attend Tony Robbins' seminar called "Unleash the Power Within." I knew I had to be at this event. Something inside of me said, "Do whatever it takes to get to this event, David." Call it a "gut feeling," but I just knew I had to be there.

I asked Peter and Adam if they could pay for me in advance to attend the event, and I promised I'd pay them back out of my salary each week. It was putting myself into another "financial hassle" I didn't need, although my gut feeling told me I just had to do it.

I flew down to see Tony Robbins and made some totally crazy commitments to myself while I was there live at the event. I even wrote these commitments into the book I was given at the event and read them out to myself when I returned home to the Gold Coast.

"Get out of the relationship you're currently in... buy a brand-new car... stop focusing on helping everyone else and start looking after yourself for once in your life... leave Peter and Adam and speak on stages all around the world, teaching people how to make money online and offline."

Once I re-read everything I wrote, I thought I must have been delusional, and I wondered how in the world would I ever accomplish one of these far-fetched goals? (Let alone accomplish them all.)

Massive Action

I took massive action and made sure I put my heart and soul into achieving my goals and outcomes, which I wrote in my book. I knew I needed to do whatever it took at the time to "become the David I knew I could become" once I took and implemented everything with massive action.

Was it hard? Yes, it was extremely difficult. There were numerous times I felt like giving up, but giving up was what I'd always done, so it wasn't an option for me anymore. I'd given up, failed, and quit way too many times in the past, so it was time for change for the better. Have you ever done this before?

Am I glad I took massive action to achieve my goals and come out bigger and better on the other side? You better believe it! I'm extremely happy— it's made my life much better in so many ways. Ways in which I could never write about on paper.

Today, I'm married to Nisarat Cavanagh who is the best wife in the World for me. She treats me like a King, and I treat her like a Queen. We never argue or fight. We choose to understand each other and talk things through. To me, it's a marriage made in Heaven, and God sent me one of his Angels.

I'm blessed with a wonderful daughter Krystal who lives on the Gold Coast of Australia, and two beautiful daughters, Pannipa and Fahsai who live with Nisarat and I in Thailand. I have three daughters who I love very much (plus a grandson named Julius and a granddaughter named Annabella).

Up until COVID time, I traveled the world teaching people how to make money online and offline. I've spoken at most of the World's biggest Internet seminars, workshops, and events as a keynote speaker. I've been voted Best Speaker at a lot of the seminars I've spoken at, which I'm very proud of.

I run 8, 10 and 12-day internet marketing workshops in Pattaya Beach, Thailand with Roger Bourdon and Bronwyn Mitchell (my coaching team) as well as my wife and business partner Nisarat Cavanagh with students flying in from all over the world to attend.

Who would have thought back then that David Cavanagh would change so much and be able to achieve all of these amazing results?

Moving Forward

You can achieve anything you want if you make a firm decision to do whatever it takes to achieve it. Think what you want, what you need to do, and then get out there and "just do it."

Secondly, you mustn't listen to people who bring you down in life. You mustn't listen to members of your family who tell you it can't be done. You need to start hanging out with people who truly care for you and your success and well-being.

Thirdly, you must take massive action and do everything within your power to achieve your goals, dreams, and outcomes. There are no "if's" and "but's."

Fourthly, never give up. If you need extra help, ask someone. If you need a push, join a mastermind group. Contact me for advice at <u>David@DavidCavanagh.com</u> if you're stuck in a rut and feeling bad about yourself.

You must learn to listen to the "inner you" which tells you that you can do and achieve anything in life if you make a decision, take action, and do whatever it takes until it's done.

Information without implementation is just "more information." Implement whatever you know needs to be done, and remember that the only truth is the end result. It's no good talking about what you're going to do. You need to get out there and do it right now. You need to start taking action immediately.

Get the results you truly deserve! Make yourself, your family, and friends proud of the "new you"— may your life from today onwards be your best life ever. I believe in you!

About David Cavanagh

David Cavanagh is an Internet Business Coach who travels the World giving keynote speeches on how to get more leads, conversions, and sales for business owners, while teaching how to get the  "number one position" in Google and YouTube.

David is a coach and mentor to the World's best leaders, helping business owners succeed in cosmetic surgery, law, travel, dental, SEO medical and legal marketing, real estate, property development and more. He's "The Coaches Coach!" Find out how he can help you at DavidCavanagh.com.

Chapter 12: Fast Forward to Personal Reinvention | Pat Mesiti

I own a personally autographed book, *The Long Walk To Freedom*— the autobiography of Nelson Mandela. It is the story of a man who dared to have a vision for a new South Africa.

Mandela was the foster son of a Tembu chief. He grew up struggling with two worlds: the traditional culture of his tribe and the hostile reality of his white-dominated nation. His passion and vision grew out of the horrors and atrocities happening to his countrymen. Armed with fierce determination, he set a course to break down apartheid, and this led to a life in prison. But more than twenty years behind bars didn't stop his vision, and the world looked on in awe as this man made the progression from prison to presidency.

Vision & Reinvention

One of the imperatives for success in life is vision and reinvention. People who use vision, to reinvent themselves, achieve success.

Ray Kroc sold paper cups to restaurants in the 1920s and worked his way up to become a top salesman. But his vision went way beyond paper cups. He had a vision of making a big impact on the restaurant business, so he quit sales to market a machine that could mix several milkshakes at a time. **When you have a vision, opportunities come to you.** Through promoting the milkshake machines, he met the McDonald brothers, who ran a highly successful restaurant. They got talking and Ray Kroc ended up becoming their partner.

Driven by his vision, he came up with the concept of duplicating the McDonalds' restaurant on the other side of town. The two brothers opposed this, so Kroc bought the restaurant from them. Back at a time when hamburgers and chips were not an accepted meal, the pioneer began developing his empire. For the first eight years he poured all he had into the concept and saw few profits in return. But today it is a worldwide billion-dollar empire.

Ray Kroc had a vision, and he changed the world.

Walt Disney did the same. He approached 303 banks before he located one willing to finance his wild, crazy scheme to build a fun park with a cartoon mouse in a swamp area. Neil Armstrong, the first man to walk on the moon, said that ever since he was a boy, he'd had a vision of doing something important in aviation.

To be a successful person, regardless of your age, you must have a vision of where you want to be. Vision will cause you to be stretched far beyond the abilities you currently possess. It will launch you into abilities you don't have right now.

Will there be pain along the way? You bet. But betterment by its very nature is about vision, and being a better person is worth the pain it takes to get there.

An athlete has a vision for gold. A businessperson has a vision for success and profits. A mother has a vision for bringing up well-balanced children in a happy family. What is your vision for life?

139

Achievable, Challenging & Worthwhile Target

In the book *Vision, Values and Courage*, Neil Snider, James Dowd and Diane Morse-Houghton say: "Vision must provide a clear image of a desirable future. One that represents an achievable, challenging, and worthwhile long-range target."

Vision isn't a goal. It's a picture, a canvas on which you paint your future. It shows you what the future could and should look like. The businessperson's canvas shows them standing in front of a tall modern building with their company name on it— a sign of their success. The athlete's painting shows them standing on the dais holding up the gold medal, surrounded by cheering fans. And a young man wanting to win the heart of his sweetheart envisions himself at the altar with his beautiful bride.

Commitment to vision is an awesome power. If you decide to persistently move towards your vision over days, weeks, months or even years, you will change your life, the lives of people around you, and your world. Regardless of setbacks.

Have you ever seen a successful athlete suffer injury and then come back to win the prize? A failed businessperson starting over again from zero to become a huge success? A husband and wife coming back from a failed marriage to build a solid, secure family unit? **These things happen because the vision stayed alive despite their circumstances.**

If you have a vision, it eases the pain when you face problems. They lose some of their sting. The vision lifts you above the difficulties and gives you strength to persevere through them and out the other side.

Once you are clear about your vision, you can reinvent yourself if your old self no longer serves you.

I have a friend who mastered the art of personal reinvention, but she wasn't always like that. She was bright at school, but her father was a military man — the family moved constantly. She dropped out of school in Year Ten, failing to adjust to a new school.

Before she got married, she did administration jobs. Then, she spent years at home looking after children. When her children were in primary school, she studied aged care and got a job in a nursing home. She studied social work, and before she'd completed her degree, secured a job working with the terminally ill. My friend loves this job. She gets to support and help individuals and their families at a daunting time. Now my friend is working full-time, caring for a family and doing a part time course on helping the hearing impaired. She is inspirational. Can you reinvent yourself even when you're juggling family and work commitments? My friend says yes, and here is some advice from her on how to do it.

The Five Steps to Personal Reinvention & Ultimate Freedom

Be realistic. Sit down and count how many hours of work and learning you need to do, and whether this will fit around your home, life, and work duties. Be realistic when making this calculation. Manage your time well.

Plan ahead. You don't want to find yourself over committed and jeopardize both your existing career and personal life. To successfully reinvent yourself, you will need to carefully put a plan together. My friend recommends finding a quiet and comfortable place to work towards to learn or study where you won't be distracted or interrupted.

Schedule time for fun. You need time to work, rest and play. You will burn yourself out if you don't make time for friends, family, and leisure time (like walks on the beach and trips to the movies). However, you need to come up with a schedule to balance work, learning new skills and family, and deliver on all fronts! But if your timetable is not working for you, be prepared to re-work it and shift items around. Consider leaving home an hour earlier a couple times a week and doing course reading in a coffee shop. Make it work for you, your team, and your family.

Ask for support when you need it. Don't try to be superman or superwoman. If you are finding the workload hard, ask friends or family for help. Friends may be your best form of support. Could anyone get some groceries or buy some frozen meals for you when you run out of time? Can you cut down your work hours? Can you hire help if you are overloaded?

The biggest advantage to continue working while you work towards reinventing yourself is that you still have an income coming in. Also, you are not stepping out of the workforce and damaging your career, and if the new skills you develop relate to your work, you are getting real-world experience. You can apply what you are learning to your current profession.

Working while learning new skills can be a win-win situation, but it can also be a lose-lose situation if you become exhausted and underperform at work and your new project.

Balancing work, learning, family and leisure time is tricky. Some people will be able to manage it, others won't. Ask yourself how much you want it? What are you willing to sacrifice? What sort of support do you have around you?

Also, you ensure the timing is right. If reinventing yourself means the world to you, explore how you can make it happen. Start the process to reinvent yourself through further learning.

About Pat Mesiti

Pat Mesiti is a self-made multi-millionaire, gifted speaker, entrepreneur, mindset growth strategist, bestselling author, and consultant.

Pat's passion is to EQUIP and EMPOWER you to experience growth and prosperity to your fullest potential. His expertise is to SHIFT MINDSETS AND TO BUILD BIGGER PEOPLE to produce results.

Free Audio Training Valued at $97 reveals: "How to think like a millionaire... and uncover the fortune that lies hidden in your mind." Claim your Free Gift from Pat at Mesiti.com/freegift.

Printed in Great Britain
by Amazon

7dd4d2da-b797-47fc-a045-3e423dd81e12R01